Peace Is Here:
CHRISTMAS REFLECTIONS

by

21904

JARS OF CLAY

WRITTEN BY JARS OF CLAY
ILLUSTRATIONS AND BOOK DESIGN BY CHRISTIE LITTLE

©2007 Gray Matters

Published by Gray Matters.
Administered by Nettwerk Productions,
1650 W. 2nd Avenue, Vancouver, BC Canada V6J 4R3

Library of Congress Cataloging-in-Publication Data on file.
Library and Archives Canada Cataloguing in Publication

Jars of Clay (Musical group)
Peace Is Here : Christmas Reflections / Jars of Clay ; illustrations by Christie Little.

Includes bibliographical references.
ISBN 1-894160-08-8

1. Advent--Meditations. 2. Christmas--Meditations. I. Little, Christie II. Title.

BV40.J37 2007   242'.33   C2007-904325-9

9-781894-160087
Printed in Canada.

This book is dedicated to everyone who still
finds awe and wonder in the story of Christmas.
And to the children of the world who believe
in stories about flying reindeer, angels
singing to shepherds, kings kneeling
in horse barns, and especially the one
about the God of the Universe
taking the form of a child....
You teach us how to believe.

TABLE OF CONTENTS

WELCOME

It is hard to understand in our food and flesh, metal-ed and motored, culturally saturated minds that Paradise is real, but it is God's reality, and his home. Without any understanding of what Paradise is like, we can't really appreciate Christ's appearance on earth.

I can only dream about what that moment was like. Although it doesn't fit my Sunday school image of angels, I've always wondered if they didn't break a rule or two that night with the shepherds. In an effort to make a secret, humble entrance, I can only imagine strict instructions going out to not blow the child's cover. I picture very antsy angels wanting mankind to know the significance of this moment. Maybe there was a negotiation...just one town. Just let us tell one town. Just one synagogue, please? Okay, what about those shepherds? We won't be loud. Just a few of us will go.

GLORIA! How could they help themselves? Men, women, listen to us, goodwill is coming from God! PEACE IS ON ITS WAY!

"....he appeared and the soul felt its worth..."

What is the worth of your soul? Christmas. Not the paper and boxed, tinseled and twinkling commercially motivated Christmas, but the Emanuel embarking on a long journey far from his Paradise to know you Christmas.

I hope in this book, through these reflections, you will be reminded of the value of your own soul. Merry Christmas.

by Sara Groves

PEACE IS HERE

Little children born to chaos,
Sojourn by the stars appear
Tho' your fears wrap all around you
Love has come and peace is here

Men to men in violent rapture
Wars lay sons in fields unknown
Hope to quell the disappointment
Justice born and mercy shown

Gloria, gloria, peace is here
Gloria, gloria peace is here

Angels sing in righteous envy,
Kings of earth kneel by the throne
Born to push against the Fall
Far as the curse is found

Gloria, gloria, peace is here
Gloria, gloria, peace is here

by Dan Haseltine

THE MATCHSTICK PROMISE

I saw an animated version of Hans Christian Andersen's story of "The Little Matchstick Girl" as a child, and I remember being pretty disturbed at the ending. It was a shockingly sad ending, and it felt like something didn't go as planned. Someone had to have forgotten some details in the story, it seemed to me. The story was incomplete.

Part of that incompleteness is something I still struggle with today. I want life to be right, right now. The girl in the story couldn't catch a break. If she wasn't out selling the matches, she'd be beaten at home by her father. If she was out selling the matches, she was going to freeze to death. Not much of a win/win scenario, I thought.

When she started lighting the matches to stay alive, she saw images of beautiful things: promises of warmth, a feast, a tall Christmas tree with candles, and finally a vision of a loved one that knew her.

Richard Rohr says all great spirituality is about what we do with our pain. That's what strikes me today. In that moment of hanging on, seeing all of the façades of safety stripped down to the bare brokenness of life, the true promises come into focus.

The circumstances of Christ's birth would not indicate that peace on earth was even a possibility, but His birth in a chaotic world was all that many had to believe in for the promised hope. In the hardship of her story, the Little Matchstick Girl saw just a vision of it on this side of life, yet that probably made it all the more beautiful when her faith became sight. As a believer in Christ's story, I have to be tuned in to the heart's longing for that completion.

by Stephen Mason

LIFE AS ADVENT

"For we know that the whole creation has been groaning
together in the pains of childbirth until now."

ROMANS 8:22

Every Christmas I'm reminded of the longing I felt growing up
as I would anticipate this special day. And while I recognize that
I was more excited about opening gifts than anything else, the
longing is still appropriate. The days leading up to Christmas-
Advent, or "waiting"—are about anticipation, reflection, feeling
the weight of the Coming of the Christ-child. And though we
immerse ourselves in the spiritual practice of waiting, we know
that Jesus has already come. It's this tension that we live in; the
in-between, the already and the not yet.

This season of Advent is a reminder of the broader groaning and anticipation we experience all life-long, for the restoration of this broken world. The Christian journey is a long-term advent—a patient longing for renewal and destination, for Restoration, when there is finally no curse and our souls are at rest. However, lest we feel like we are stuck in a waiting room, remember that Emmanuel means God With Us. Christ has come, and we have a present peace and assurance through Him. May the hope of God-becoming-man bring us strength and joy today as we wait amidst the brokenness of this "groaning world." May the Peace of Jesus bring light to the darkness that threatens to overwhelm.

by Charlie Lowell

CHILD OF SORROWS

"A cry of anguish is heard in Ramah–
weeping and mourning unrestrained
Rachel weeps for her children,
Refusing to be comforted–for they
Are dead."

Matthew 2:18

The road to Egypt wound through the desert like a trickle of blood, thick and silent. Their eyes wore rings of salt and the night air said nothing and everything all at once. This was the way that prophets had foretold, John had prepared and angels had announced. But as soon as their joy had come it was silenced.

Rachel weeps.

She weeps for the genocide at Christmas. What an impossibly confusing start to God's story of renewal, a bloody and dark pronouncement along with the hope of the world.

My steps in Rwanda are the closest I have ever taken to witnessing genocide. I pray that it's as close as I ever get. The yawning holes left behind by whole demographics systematically removed are startling at first, numbing the next and finally exhale into a daily devastation. I wonder if Jesus was an anomaly among his own people, a heartbreaking reminder of all those that had been lost to Herod: a holocaust survivor. It was to this generation acquainted with sorrow and grief that he would later dare to proclaim, "Blessed are those who mourn, for they will be comforted." And it was among their tattered and grief stricken hearts that his message took root. So if this Christmas you find yourself, like the people of Rwanda, shaken by the evil God's people do to one another, take heart with Rachel. God still is and has always been near the broken. His message is still going out and taking root amongst those in desperate need as it did nearly two thousand years ago. And for the rest of us, thanks be to God for the babe who would one day become the "man of sorrows."

by Matt Odmark

OH CHRISTMAS TREE

When I was little, one of my favorite traditions was to put some Christmas records on and sneak down under the Christmas tree and stare up through the branches. If I squinted my eyes until they were nearly closed, the lights would swirl together. It was beautiful and peaceful, and most nights in December I fell asleep under the tree as the sounds of John Denver and the Muppets faded. Growing up, I never had a real Christmas tree. My parents owned a fake tree, having heard about the dangers that went along with keeping a dry tree wrapped in hundreds of tiny hot lights in a stand in a living room. I didn't really appreciate their logic. Our tree was only ever in danger of melting and sticking to the chocolate brown shag carpet; that seemed like a much greater problem than vacuuming up stray pine needles.

My family Christmas tree was not a cool fake tree like the ones with aluminum branches and a color wheel. Our tree was supposed to look real, but it didn't. Every year we screwed the post together, laid all the

color-coded branches out on the floor, and began the process of assembly. Once it was erected, we bent the branches to remove all evidences of the box where it had lain entombed since last mid-January.

I always admired people who had real Christmas trees. When someone took the time to drag a real tree into their house, they said something about their risk tolerance and courage level. As a fan of Indiana Jones, and Luke Skywalker, I was whole-heartedly an advocate for those people. People with real trees were adventurous—skirting danger, and bucking the doomsayers who flung about tragic statistics of house fires and charred toys and gifts.

Mostly, I loved the aroma. There was something fresh and wonderful about the smell of real pine, evergreen or spruce. It was very different than the sprays and candles my mother would use as equal parts denial and illusion. In the late seventies and early eighties the scientists that worked in such fields had not perfected the "real Christmas tree" smell. It was problematic. When people came to my house, they smelled pine air freshener, saw plastic and metal branches. Then I felt the same way I did when my mom bought me fake parachute pants to wear to school instead of the name brand ones that all the cool kids were wearing. At night, though, I still had my tradition; that never changed.

My first Christmas in my own house marked a kind of liberation. I spent way too much money on a beautiful white Spruce. It was too big for my living room, but I decorated it. I breathed deeply and let the smell of real Christmas tree fill my nostrils. After putting on, *A Muppet's Family Christmas*, I lay down, squinted my eyes to see the colored lights glimmer, and fell asleep. I woke up years later, at the beginning of December, with children of my own. This year we will light a few pine-scented candles, pull the Christmas tree down from the attic, lay out the color-coded branches, and assemble the family Christmas tree. If things go my way, hopefully we can all curl up under it and fall asleep.

by Dan Haseltine

AN UNBREAKABLE THREAD

This year on Father's day my adopted son came home to my wife and I. He is our first and only child. There has never been nor will there ever be another day in my life like that one. Like most roads to adoption, ours was a twisted and heart-wrenching one. There were so many near-misses and so many devastations along the way that we were just sure our spirits would break beyond the point of recovery. How could such a fragile hope as ours survive such a dangerous journey? Yet somehow he is here and he is no small miracle. You need only look into his black-brown eyes to fall headlong into a deep, deep well, where heartache and joy co-mingle and overwhelming sadness and unshakeable hope hold hands. It is in both the possibility and reality of his new, new life that all the hopelessly contrary fragments of my own life seem to become only extremes in the vibrations of an unbreakable thread, solidly resonating with the music of everything.

And he is just a boy.

So Christmas will become new to us this year, and not just in the obvious ways. For we will never look on the last hope of God and men placed into the adoptive care of a decent but simple Jew and his teenage bride the same way again. Our hearts will beat with a fresh ache for the thread of sadness that those two willingly allowed to be sewn into their lives. A thread that would cost them dearly, and that many people would never understand. In the face of this, the music of my life sings in a new way and reveals the possibility that one day, that thread might weave a redemption that will catch the whole world.

by Matt Odmark

IT'S EASIER TO GIVE

My culture and my Bible have taught me, from earliest childhood, that it is better to give than receive. A strange elixir of pride and humility, there is nothing that brings me that sense of satisfaction as when I'm able to provide for someone in need. I've even started seeing it in my own children. Recently one of my sons said, "Daddy, it makes me feel so good when I give something to someone!" I think it's a beautiful side of our humanity to want to share what we have with others. But there's also a problem. Giving tends to feed a selfish hero-complex that lurks within us. We want to rescue, to hand down and help out. We want to be strong, independent and in control.

For us, receiving comes a little harder, doesn't it? It implies weakness, dependency, and need. These are not characters that our culture holds in high regard. We are trained to earn our keep, and not accept handouts. The idea of grace is offensive to our rational minds. William Willimon makes the point that, "the Christmas story...is not about how blessed it is to be givers but about how essential it is to see ourselves as receivers." In the biblical Christmas narrative, our only role is to receive. We respond by welcoming the Christ-Child and crying, "Thanks be to God for this indescribable gift!" And, "Emmanuel! God is with us!"

Maybe it is better to give, but only after we have truly identified ourselves as receivers. We need to learn how to be humble recipients of God's gift before we can turn around and offer a gift to anyone else. Our first priority must be that we see ourselves as rescued from exile. Are we willing to see ourselves as needy? As receivers of great gifts? Only then we can turn and offer this gift of Grace to others with the true giving heart of God.

by Charlie Lowell

WILLIMON, WILLIAM. ORIGINALLY PRINTED IN DECEMBER 21-28, 1998 P. 1173 ISSUE OF THE CHRISTIAN CENTURY. MT. MORRIS, ILLINOIS © 1988 CHRISTIAN CENTURY FOUNDATION.

CHRISTMAS REBELLION

"Count not thyself to have found true peace,
if thou hast felt no grief; nor that then all is well if thou hast no adversary;
nor that this is perfect, if all things fall out according to thy desire."

–THOMAS A. KEMPIS

Christmas is a time for God's people boldly to be seen as those who have given themselves over to notions of peace on earth and good will toward mankind. They are either naive notions, or sentiments born of complete ignorance, especially in the wake of such obvious worldly realities as perpetual war and present violence toward humanity. So, WHICH IS IT?

When it appears that humanity has found the business of violence most inspiring, we who follow Jesus sound the horns of goodness and compassion. When humanity is most hungry to act out the most brutal forms of oppression, we ring the bells of peace and charity. It is

21904

the stuff of lunatic minds. *Or is it?* The Spirit of Christmas sets upon us in the midst of chaos and destruction, and gives us a voice to cry, "Good Will!" or "Peace on earth!" This is an act of rebellion! A full-forced movement against the effects of the Fall. It is not blind faith, nor is it childish rhetoric. It is holy wisdom. And it is as out of place as a host of angels hovering above a band of shepherds. It is as rebellious an occurrence as the intrusion of joy and the fullness of life manifested in the heart and mind and soul of a man laid on the torture table for his beliefs. The Christmas Spirit means to stir the hearts of all humanity, and it means to offend the rational and common-sensical mind. If there is any naive notion at large during the Christmas season, it is one that characterizes the Spirit of this time as merely cheerful and warm.

by Dan Haseltine

First Baptist Church Arnold
2012 Missouri State Rd.
Arnold, Mo 63010

A GIFT OF DARKNESS

When the angel Gabriel suddenly appeared to Mary, her first response was fear and "troubling." (LUKE 29) I wonder these days how much I would stake on a visit from an angel. Was it a dream? An angelic apparition? What would my family and friends think if I told them? The angel's "Good News" would certainly change Mary's life, and she accepted it with grace and humility. But I can imagine that she spent many days and nights in terror and doubt; whether she was really chosen by God, and destined to birth His immaculate Son! While this news brought joy and purpose for Mary, there was on some level a death involved. She was forging new ground, leaving the 'old Mary' behind. Luci Shaw suggests that Mary was given a "gift of darkness" from the angel. There was an inherent bittersweetness in Gabriel's message.

My biggest struggle with faith and love is the constant and daily call to abandon myself. It's contrary to my nature to sacrifice for others. The journey of faith is, not unlike Mary's first moments with the angel, terrifying and troubling. It most certainly embodies new life and hope, but this comes at a cost. We no longer live for ourselves, but find our purpose in weakness and service. The beauty breaks through when we are able to accept the pain and sorrow of leaving ourselves behind. What awaits us is an unparalleled joy and fulfillment in this new identity. Our lives mimic Mary in that we give birth to Grace and Hope in a world overcome with pain. The old is gone, and the new has come. Suddenly the gift of darkness gives way to growth and purpose as we see ourselves as a very small part of God's coming Kingdom.

by Charlie Lowell

REFERENCE: "WINTER SONG," CHRISTMAS READINGS BY MADELEINE L'ENGLE AND LUCI SHAW
© 1996 BY HAROLD SHAW PUBLISHERS

A GIFT OF MILLIONS

My son asked me last Christmas if they have Christmas in Africa. "Why doesn't Santa stop there?" It was a hard truth he innocently stumbled on. In the moment, I didn't feel anything but sadness and an overwhelming feeling that I should have an answer.

I'm starting to ask questions when I don't know how to respond. Maybe to get more clues. So, I asked him what he thought about it...it wasn't much of a father-knows-best moment. I don't know that we figured anything out. And that's probably what truly was good about the exchange.

The lack of answers exposed that simply in the discussion we honor millions of people's stories. Not ignoring it, nor running away from it, but keeping it on the grid of people and things we are connected to, and in which we are graciously implicated. A very present questioning and suffering that would singularly point to hope through Christ's birth.

It was a question that led my son and I to consider an idea of justice in the world that we both could understand and share together. *That might have been the best gift he gave me that Christmas.*

by Stephen Mason

THE BURDEN OF HOPE

*"But Mary treasured up all these things
and pondered them in her heart."*

LUKE 2:19

Christmas comes each year with its dangerous invitation to hope. Yet for most of us this invitation feels more like an inconvenience and a burden. In our busy-ness, we consider the burden of Christmas ourselves, even as Mary herself pondered the meaning of all of these things. I wonder how many of her personal hopes and dreams were on the altar at this moment. Surely this was not the life that she had dreamed for herself, and who could possibly understand the road that she was about to walk? Who would go with her? As she began to consider all that she would lose along the way, the invitation to hope must have felt callous and farfetched. If you are like me, this is where most of my adult Christmases have been spent, burdened and heavy under the Hope that promises much but asks for everything along the way. Maybe this is your story this year; maybe your losses have been deep and painful. Maybe you stand in the reality of every Christmas from now on being a bitter reminder of those that are no longer with you. You grieve things that have been lost along the way. If this is you, take courage from Mary, who somehow found a way to move from deep pondering and introspection to singing. Singing! Somewhere along the road the question of her life ceased to be "If you knew me and loved me, God, how could you ask this of me" to "God, who do you see when you look at me?" Somewhere along the way her hope was unfettered from all those good things that she had hoped her life would be and became anchored to God's hopes for her.

> *"For he has been mindful of the humble state of his servant.*
> *From now on all generations will call me blessed,"*

Luke 2:48

by Matt Odmark

THE SHARED STORY

Mondays over the last three years, I've been meeting with a group of men of varying ages and backgrounds. First, we've reaffirmed the truth of the gospel story. Next, we've heard together what that means for us, as natural loners who recognize the dangers of isolation, as natural wanderers who are finding peace at home, as natural liars who are finding freedom in the truth, as natural judges who are learning to judge ourselves aright, and as natural strongmen who are experiencing God's strength as we admit our weakness. Finally, having heard of God, we each tell our story and we locate God and God's people in it.

This random group has developed into a community of brothers who are learning that life can't be figured out or lived alone. We've learned that who we want to become—who each wants to become—is constructed communally, by submitting to others in God's community.

We have a Monday meeting around Christmas, even when the church is closed. We meet in the foyer, lit only by a huge Christmas tree with white lights. It's more reverent than other meetings throughout the year. I believe that's partly because the birth of Christ is a common denominator to every man, woman, and child who wants to understand their own story in its sadness and brokenness, and the longing to see it one day fully redeemed.

Not only has God given us each a story that is uniquely one's own, He has also seen fit in the story of Jesus' birth, represented in that church as a glowing white Christmas tree, to remind us of what is consistent in all of our stories.

It is the light by which we see and experience our own lives in truth. What we long for as our own story's end will come to be because of the birth of a child.

by Stephen Mason

'NOT WHAT WE WANTED!

"... because of the tender mercy of our God, whereby the sunrise shall visit us from on high to give light to those who sit in darkness and in the shadow of death, to guide our feet into the way of peace."

FROM ZECHARIAH'S PROPHECY OF THE BIRTH OF CHRIST,
IN LUKE 1:78, 79....

Jews were taught to wait for a warrior king that would come in power to fulfill the prophecies of the Old Testament. When Jesus came as a vulnerable baby, it confused and angered political and religious leaders of the day. The mystery of divine nature is a baby!? Life and faith were suddenly turned upside down. This reality challenged what Jewish Scripture expected and waited for.

I think that most days we still desire a different sort of King than Jesus. Some days we want a powerful warrior King. At other times we just want a best friend that will look out for our interests. The last thing I want to do is to surrender my desires and sacrifice my precious time. I don't want to step out and risk loving messy people, or spending time with someone very different than myself. In most practical ways, these ideals seem like a waste of time. But Jesus breaks into our world challenging everything we take for granted. God's Son brings new possibilities. My possessions are not mine. My enemies deserve my love. The last shall be first. It's not a race to see who gets there first. The purpose is found in the journey, as we walk and struggle and learn to love.

Wouldn't it be easier to navigate this life if Jesus were a warrior King? On our more honest days, we can confess that we are still waiting for something else. And yet, as we look longer at Jesus, something in us clicks. It is in our fabric to love. *Our souls do crave peace.* As we surrender to this Child born to teach us the way of peace, we become more capable of living in this upside-down Kingdom.

by Charlie Lowell

FIRST BREATH

Have you ever taken a walk in the snow at the time of night when cars have stopped their frequent passing? The windows of neighborhood houses show that people have settled in; all the rooms are dark, with only electric candles and twinkling lights on artificial trees showing until the crispness of morning air arrives to usher in another day nearer to Christmas.

I love walking outside on cold winter nights. The geese and squirrels of fall have gone, and the robins and cardinals of spring have not arrived. There is no echo, for nothing escapes the porous blanket of white that keeps all sound from reverberating.

In the silence, a person can hear the beating of a heart, the gentle rhythm of breathing, the cadence of footsteps and quite possibly, nothing else.

The evidences of stirring hopeful life are almost entirely covered. But below the surface is a youthful anticipation—time is moving forward, and the world, although quiet, is not frozen and still, it simply waits. Like a child staring up into the sky on Christmas Eve, no words need be spoken; the mind, heart, and gut are full of anticipation that needs no outward voice.

The world is waiting to celebrate the day when hope and love and justice drew first breath, took root and forced the process of a first thaw. Christmas Day is the beginning of a story; the birth of good, right and just things that have weight and purpose.

This birth of a child as the means for the intrusion of peace, the end of unbridled chaos and reigning fear does not make sense. It confounds anyone with a bent toward logic. Yet there is nothing to lose from the inclusion of wonderment and awe, toward a God who builds stories that rest on the shoulders of failed underdogs and least-likely saints.

The earth waits for Christmas, because it is part of the creation that reminds us all that ours is a story being written; a story of love, heroes, tragedies, and victories. A story as true as snow is white, and as biting in its telling, as the winter wind skating across a northern plain.

Where do we see ourselves in the chorus of waiting life? Are we under the blankets of family dysfunction, grief, loss, cold-heartedness, and fear—all as porous and capable of silencing life as the deep snows? Where do we find a connection to the hopeful anticipation of peace, hope, justice and joy? We are not apart from the story of peace entering into chaos, we are both collective and individual examples of this. We may even be privileged to be conduits of it.

By Dan Haseltine

GOOD NEWS FOR WHOM?

"And the angel said to them,
'Fear not, for behold, I bring you good news of a great joy
that will be for all the people.'"

LUKE 2:10

Who would have thought that the Glory of God would be delivered into poverty and dirt! The Son of God belonged in a palace, on a throne—certainly anywhere but a stable. Jesus entered this world vulnerable and with no material glory. The blue-collared shepherds were the first to see the star and follow. Throughout Jesus' life, He is constantly challenging the powerful and identifying with the weak and poor. The political and religious leaders were consistently angered by Jesus' words and actions, but it was always good news for the poor—the broken, the discouraged, the sick and homeless. His message was always full of hope and healing for those in need. How are we poor—if not financially, are we poor in spirit—humbled by our unworthiness of God's good gifts to us? The comfortable and successful have little need for a Savior. How might we submit ourselves to this love, realizing that it is more powerful than our personal kingdoms, our wish lists, our career choices? How might we submit to this love that can alone bring light and life to someone else? Jesus is building a Kingdom, and love alone is the key to His city.

"Blessed are the poor in spirit, for theirs is the kingdom of heaven."
Matthew 5:3

(untitled)
by Oscar Romero

No one can celebrate
a genuine Christmas
without being truly poor.
The self-sufficient, the proud,
those who, because they have
everything, look down on others,
those who have no need
even of God—for them there
will be no Christmas.

Only the poor, the hungry,
those who need someone
to come on their behalf,
will have that someone.
That someone is God.
Emmanuel. God-with-us.
Without poverty of spirit
there can be no abundance of God.

by Charlie Lowell

THE THINGS THAT HAVE BEEN HANDED DOWN

The North Shore of Minnesota in December is like a monument to winter. The naked birch trees stand white on white against the snow that has been accumulating since September. The din of Lake Superior's steadily droning waves has been muted by more than a half a mile of gray ice and snow. Winter comes with such force and authority that everything bows to its demands. Businesses shut down, roads close, cars become less reliable means of transportation than snowmobiles and walking, and entire towns collectively yawn as all memories of summer activity drown in a blanket of white.

This was the childhood Eden that was my Grandparents' home. I was there for Christmas only twice. It was not a lack of familial closeness that kept us a way as much as mileage. My Grandfather passed away this year and so I have found myself caught up in the memories of those Christmases we did have, and especially to the gifts that they left behind. As is often the case, the most-cherished gifts that my Grandparents gave me never found their way underneath a Christmas tree. But if they were to ever make it on a list it would be as follows:

1. *A summer spent building log cabins, forts and other shared adventures*
2. *An appreciation for beauty and wilderness*
3. *The joy of showing kindness*
4. *An always-full stomach*
5. *The beauty of living small, simply and with deference to others*
6. *A willingness to live in God's plans with a humble acceptance*
7. *A life lived without unfinished business.*

May you find the time to pause and thank God for the things that he has handed down to you this Christmas. Things you won't find under the tree.

by Matt Odmark

THE GRISWOLDIAN AGE:

(A SATIRE, TO BE READ WITH THE STOIC SCOTTISH INFLECTION
OF WILLIAM WALLACE OR SHREK)

We have journeyed a great distance from the ways of aluminum trees and color wheels. We have taken giant leaps forward, above and beyond the hollowed plastic Santas that stood frozen alongside translucent reindeer poised on the verge of meltdown each night as they splayed their soft glow.

For those of us who take seriously one of the last great conduits for evoking Christmas Spirit in and around our homes and neighborhoods, we have come to a new age. We now have robotic reindeer, and animatronic nativity scenes with their own short wave radio broadcasting capabilities. The technological advancements in the field of holiday home decorating have given us all reason to believe again. And yet in the light of such advancements like these, we see the ruin and erosion of this high art all around us. We should have known it would happen. Every great art form has its masters and its imposters.

Icicle lights, not the ones that fall gracefully like drops of pure snow-light, but the ones that hold that zig-zag, "just de-rubberbanded" look, spill across the front gutters of cape style homes across America. This is a mockery, and I am offended. For example, take those bushes carelessly draped in "square Christmas light nets." Have we ushered in the birth of this new and inspiring age, only to fall prey to the convenience of such horrors as this? Do people think they can get away with simply flinging a web of lights across a bush, as if it were a two-hundred-pound hound dog forced to wear the sweater of a toy poodle? We can not allow such activities to continue. Because we are artists, we will seek out only the best laser light shows that spell out the nicest holiday phrases. We must display only the biggest inflatable snowmen, and in places where snow does not fall, we will use only the whitest and purest forms of cotton fiber to spread around our palm trees and crab grass lawns. We will do all of this because a little child was born in a manger. Because angels revealed a great message of hope to shepherds, it is our job to mirror that "host of heaven" effect with strobes and chase light sequences choreographed to the best rock n' roll renditions of Christmas classics we can find on the internet. THIS IS OUR TIME! THIS IS THE GRISWOLDIAN AGE!

by Dan Haseltine

WHO GETS TO BE SANTA?

It's been an emerging role in my Christmas story. Santa. As a child, there were years of tearing into presents as fast as I could. I hardly remember looking up from the present before me, and I see that same glee in the wide-eyed, eager faces of my kids now. We become intent on nothing but what is before us. It's all about receiving. As an adult (in most respects), I'm finally comprehending the other side of the exchange, and started to appreciate my place in the role of the Santa.

Giving a gift initiates something inside us that says that in this great big world, we can wield a small piece of the power to restore, encourage, and love. *We can be the giver.* These gifts, even in small practice, have large implications for our heart, mind, soul and body. I believe this is significant because in learning to be givers we mimic the story of the Gospel, and the echoes of redemption.

I'm reading some contemplative writers these days, and they all seem to capture a similar thought, "to gain our life is to first lose it, so give it over." And the crazy thing is, this is how I experience life in those moments of giving gifts away. I gain life! Purpose, fulfillment, and most importantly, love comes quickly.

Like one of the great contemplatives of old, Dr. Seuss's Grinch discovered the truth, too. *The heart swells many times larger as a result of giving.*

by Stephen Mason

HIBERNATION DAY

It seems that for me and most of my friends the one gift that we hope for every Christmas and rarely get is rest. Especially as our families and responsibilities grow our bodies cry out for it, and we promise ourselves each Christmas season that it is just around the next bend like the delicious carrot on that cartoon stick. But most of us crash into the new year with the discouraged realization that we are more tired and in need of a vacation than our recent vacationing provided. We long for a day to hibernate, stay inside, and find reprieve from our to-do lists and responsibilities. To allow the slinky-toy effect of our existence to recoil, so our soul can finally catch up and once again take residence in our body. A day to be present in the world, quiet and still enough to hear the sound of our one, singular life in close quarters with those that we love.

In Nashville where I live, we don't hide from the cold of winter as much as we hibernate in our air conditioning during the brutal summer months to avoid the perma-sweat of ninety degree days and one-hundred-percent humidity. It is during one of these freon-fueled inspired hibernations that I write today. Our newborn son is only two weeks home, and my wife and I are still happily in the haze of days spent in a fog of coffee and interrupted sleep, with nothing in the world as important as being there for what our son might do next. The pressures of work and the responsibilities of life and friends have been temporarily lifted, and we enjoy our right as first time parents to simply be where we are and nowhere else. I can not remember the last time life was so singular and coherent, and I thank God for this reprieve.

I know that the responsibilities of life are looming, and will be back soon with their lists of demands and expectations. And I am even more aware than I have ever been what courage and determination it takes to truly rest in today's world. This is no small thing, and only gets more difficult as the years go by. But I hope that this Christmas we can all find the courage to find a day or two to simply hibernate in peace and enjoy the view from inside.

by Matt Odmark

NEXT CHRISTMAS

There was a Christmas in my childhood that ended with a red face. I didn't receive the one gift I'd expected, and I was feeling sorry for myself. It was the "Red Rider BB Gun" that never showed up. As I look back on that, I'm reminded of the transitions I have gone through in life around Christmastime.

For me, Christmas started as a time of wonder and excitement at all the things surrounding it. Soon, I went through an age where I had certain expectations. Once that happened, disappointment was frequent. I had spoiled all the glory of the experience. Other stages followed. After my parents' divorce, through adolescence, and leaving home for college, something happened in those transitions that brought me to other places.

Christmastime was evolving. *Christmas slowly became more about being together*—not just about giving and receiving gifts.

I'm seeing it all for what it is, these days. My previous experiences bring a weight to what I know now. Christmas has changed over time for me, but that's not so bad. In realizing this, I see a progress and feel a hope. In my history I "read" providence and redemption. I'm a person in process, and a work that is not yet completed. The Christmas story ties together different moments of my story, and reminds me that everything matters, and all is not without hope for change.

by Stephen Mason

ISAIAH'S TALE

"There are no rules of architecture for a castle in the clouds."
– G.K. CHESTERTON

Isaiah once told us a magical story of people living in darkness seeing light, and of people bound in slavery being freed. Within the architecture of the story lives a plot that moves us toward the end of all wars, and a wonderful declaration that peace will prevail. Hope will not leave us despairing, and though love will break us, it will not leave us in our brokenness, but restore us to the fullness of life. It is the kind of story only plausible to the mind of a child; although fantastical, it is true.

In this story there are no bounds; a child can be king of the universe, a shepherd can behold a symphony of angels, and a failed and broken people can be the object of affection for the God of all beauty. There is no evil unimagined, and no good that does not triumph over it.

*Now, where did we leave off...*OH YES, "Now the birth of Jesus Christ took place in this way...."

by Dan Haseltine

THE DISARMING CHILD

Helpless and human
Deity in the dirt,
Spirit married with flesh
We couldn't make it to you,
But you come to us.

You always come to us.
In our stubbornness and desire,
Entitlement and shame
Remind us that we need you,
Merge your untamed
Spirit with our flesh.

We try to forget those
Years of wandering.
Shackles and masters,
An eternity of doubting
And still, you come to us.

A divine intrusion
Through our scheming and chaos–
Coats of armor, angels and armies.
Do some wrecking here,
And gently come to us.

Disturb us this day
Through sorrow and through dancing,
The bliss of joy and sting of death
Past hands that would
threaten and tear,
You come to us extravagantly.

From your manger lowly,
Mighty and mysterious
You come to us, Seed of Heaven
Spirit wed with flesh,
These broken hearts to mend.

by Charlie Lowell

THE WORK OF BELIEVING

I know that for many people, winter is connected to profound sadness. It can ring dissonant with the optimism of the season's songs and stories. Yet, for children, it's largely still full of optimistic wonder. The stories, the songs, the holiday rituals. They require something that children have naturally. Simple belief. The wondrous capacity for this has long faded for many adults.

The most difficult thing I do during the holidays is believe. Believe that the beauty of this season in its spirit and story do matter, and continue to mean more as I fight for it. And it does involve an active fight in my heart.

It requires me to put off the cynical, which comes to me so easily, and choose to put on "a second naivete," as Paul Ricoeur and Karl Barth have said. A renewed, soft heart that says the Christmas story can again be good, simple, and true today. LET US BE CHILDREN AGAIN!

by Stephen Mason

I HEARD THE BELLS ON CHRISTMAS DAY

What sense do we make of this message of "Peace on earth, good will to men?" Does God's song not mock the very men and women whose lives continue to be lived out in the very real wars that keep this world on the razor's edge?

It is not enough to say that this peace is just metaphorical, or even some sort of peace of mind from which we can transcend from reality. For we do not live at the mercy of metaphorical wars. Although it may seem like it in the West. If we are rich enough, we may be able to live much of our lives using religion as nothing more than just another anti-depressant. Often faith becomes an accessory to my over-busy and self-sufficient life which I embrace only when the harshness of reality begins to encroach.

But is that all Faith is?

As I have ventured out amongst the poor of the world whether in the house churches of Vietnam and China or the villages of rural Africa, I have seen the church as a vital gathering point for those with no hope other than a God who calls things that are not as if they were. For it is the poor and those that recognize that they are no different than the poor that realize that they actually need a God who would come to them, not metaphorically but literally, naturally and supernaturally. For they live in a world that is beyond hope of repair by any other hands than the divine. And it was to them that God's message of peace went out.

MAY GOD'S VERY REAL PEACE FIND YOU TODAY.

When in despair I bowed my head
There is no peace on earth I said
For Hate is Strong and Mocks the song
Of peace on earth good Will to men

Then Peeled the Bells more Loud and Deep
God is not Dead nor doth he sleep
The wrong shall fail, the right prevail
With peace on earth good will to men.

–VERSES 4 AND 5 OF "I HEARD THE BELLS ON CHRISTMAS DAY,"
WRITTEN BY HENRY W. LONGFELLOW DURING THE VERY REAL
AMERICAN CIVIL WAR.

by Matt Odmark

BIBLIOGRAPHY

INTRODUCTION

CAPPEAU, PLACIDE. "MINUIT CHRÉTIENS," 1847. TRANSLATED FROM FRENCH TO ENGLISH BY JOHN S. DWIGHT, 1855.

STEVE

From THE WORK OF BELIEVING:

1. RICOEUR, PAUL. THE SYMBOLISM OF EVIL. BOSTON: BEACON PRESS, 1960, P. 351.
2. WALLACE, MARK I. THE SECOND NAIVETÉ: BARTH, RICOEUR AND THE NEW YALE THEOLOGY. MACON, GA: MERCER UNIVERSITY PRESS, 1990.

From THE MATCHSTICK PROMISE:

1. ROHR, RICHARD. ADAM'S RETURN: THE FIVE PROMISES OF MALE INITIATION. NEW YORK: CROSSROAD PUBLISHING, 2004.

MATT

From I HEARD THE BELLS ON CHRISTMAS DAY

1. LONGFELLOW, HENRY WADSWORTH AND CALKIN, JOHN B. "I HEARD THE BELLS ON CHRISTMAS DAY." WORDS BY HENRY WADSWORTH LONGFELLOW, 1864. MUSIC BY JOHN B. CALKIN, 1872.

From CHILD OF SORROWS:

1. NEW INTERNATIONAL VERSION, MATT. 2:18.
2. NEW INTERNATIONAL VERSION, MATT. 5:4.
3. NEW INTERNATIONAL VERSION, ISA. 53:3.

From THE BURDEN OF HOPE:

1. NEW INTERNATIONAL VERSION, LUKE 2:19.
2. NEW INTERNATIONAL VERSION, LUKE 2:48.

DAN

From ISAIAH'S TALE:
1. ENGLISH STANDARD VERSION, MATT. 2:1.

From CHRISTMAS REBELLION:
1. KEMPIS, THOMAS A. THE IMITATION OF CHRIST. NEW YORK: VINTAGE;
REV SUB EDITION, 1998.

CHARLIE

From A GIFT OF DARKNESS:
1. L'ENGLE, MADELEINE AND SHAW, LUCI. WINTERSONG: CHRISTMAS READINGS.
WHEATON, IL: HAROLD SHAW PUBLISHERS, 1996.

From NOT WHAT WE WANTED:
1. ENGLISH STANDARD VERSION, LUKE 1:78, 79.

From GOOD NEWS FOR WHOM?:
1. ENGLISH STANDARD VERSION, LUKE 2:10.
2. ENGLISH STANDARD VERSION, MATT. 5:3.
3. ROMERO, OSCAR. THE VIOLENCE OF LOVE. FARMINGTON, PA: PLOUGH, 1998.

From IT'S EASIER TO GIVE:
1. WILLIMON, WILLIAM. THE CHRISTIAN CENTURY. MT. MORRIS, IL: CHRISTIAN CENTURY
FOUNDATION, 1988.

From LIFE AS ADVENT:
1. ENGLISH STANDARD VERSION, ROM. 8:22.

ACKNOWLEDGEMNENTS

Thanks to the Rev. Joel Anderle for
your great care and wisdom in editing
these thoughts, to Sara Groves for
the introduction and to our friends
at Nettwerk Management:
Michael Corcoran, Christie Little,
Jenny Oppenheimer, Janet Weir
and Ianthe Zevos.